LEVERS

Author: David and Patricia Armentrout

Simple Machines

ROURKE PUBLISHING
Vero Beach, Florida 32964

© 2010 Rourke Publishing LLC

All rights reserved. No part of this book may be reproduced or utilized in any form or by any means, electronic or mechanical including photocopying, recording, or by any information storage and retrieval system without permission in writing from the publisher.

www.rourkepublishing.com

PHOTO CREDITS: © Mik122: Title page; © Christopher Dromey: page 04; © Roberta Casaliggi: page 05; © jpatava: page 06; © didden: page 07; © Amysuem: page 09; © JeremyRichards: page 10; © Armentrout: page 13; © Monkey Business Images: page 15; © Steve Cukrov: page 16; © Armentrout: page 17; © Xalanx: page 18; © ronnieb: page 19; © Jostein Hauge: page 20; © Masalski Maksim: page 21; © Glenda M. Powers: page 22

Edited by Kelli Hicks

Cover and Interior designed by Tara Raymo

Library of Congress Cataloging-in-Publication Data

Armentrout, David, 1962-
 Levers / David and Patricia Armentrout.
    p. cm. -- (Simple machines)
 Previous ed. by Patricia Armentrout under title: Lever.
 ISBN 978-1-60694-388-5 (hadrcover)
 ISBN 978-1-60694-520-9 (softcover)
 1. Levers--Juvenile literature. I. Armentrout, Patricia, 1960- II. Armentrout, Patricia, 1960- Lever. III. Title.
 TJ147.A763 2009
 621.8--dc22

2009006070

Rourke Publishing

www.rourkepublishing.com – rourke@rourkepublishing.com
Post Office Box 643328 Vero Beach, Florida 32964

TABLE OF CONTENTS

Machines	4
Simple and Complex	6
Lever Basics	8
First Class Levers	12
Second Class Levers	14
Third Class Levers	18
Double Levers	20
Find It, Use It	22
Glossary	23
Index	24

MACHINES

Do you know what it means when someone says, "Take a load off?" It means to rest, or take it easy. How do you take it easy when there is work to do? Simple, you use a machine to make the work easier.

Think about some machines people use everyday like bicycles, trucks, and can openers. Yes, can openers are machines! They are simple machines.

Work equals the **effort**, or force, used to move or lift something over a distance.

SIMPLE AND COMPLEX

Bicycles and trucks are **complex machines** with many moving parts. We combine different kinds of simple machines when we build complex machines.

Simple machines have few, if any, moving parts. The lever, wedge, pulley, wheel, screw, and inclined plane are simple machines. Don't be fooled by their name, though. Even though they are simple, they can still make our work easier.

A hammer is a type of lever used to drive and remove nails.

LEVER BASICS

Levers come in many forms, including can openers. But, before you learn how a can opener is a lever, you need to know some lever basics.

A lever is a strong bar that helps lift or move objects. Levers give us a **mechanical advantage**. That means they help us do work with less effort. All levers need a **load**, an effort, and a **fulcrum**. The position of the fulcrum is important when using levers.

Load—the object that moves or lifts
Effort—the force used to move or lift the object
Fulcrum—the support on which a lever turns, or rests

A long time ago, before the invention of machines, people did the heavy lifting and moving. Later, people used animals and machines like wheels and levers to help. A smart man named Archimedes lived in ancient times. He studied levers. He understood that with the right kind of lever, a person could move a great weight with a small effort. Archimedes even said that if he could find a place to stand, he could move the Earth!

Archimedes was a Greek scientist and inventor who lived more than 2,000 years ago.

FIRST CLASS LEVERS

A seesaw is a great example of a first class lever. The board of a seesaw rests on a support, which acts as a fulcrum. With all first class levers, the fulcrum lies between the load and the effort. People sitting on both ends of the seesaw are the load and effort. Effort applied to one end of the seesaw causes the person to move at the opposite end.

EFFORT

FULCRUM

LOAD

Lifting a friend is easy when you use this kind of lever.

13

SECOND CLASS LEVERS

A gardener uses a second-class lever to move tools, dirt, and mulch. What lever do they use? A wheelbarrow. A wheelbarrow is a second-class lever. On a second-class lever, the load is between the fulcrum and the effort. Imagine lifting the handles of a wheelbarrow filled with dirt. You apply the effort at one end when you lift the load in the middle. The fulcrum is the wheel that rests on the ground at the opposite end.

Wheelbarrows are useful for moving all sorts of things.

15

Can you think of another second-class lever? Think about the way a can opener works. Where are the effort, load, and fulcrum? You apply the effort at one end; the tip of the opener (the fulcrum) rests at the other end. That leaves the load in the middle where the opener grabs the lip of the can.

Remember, first class levers have the fulcrum in the middle. Second class levers have the load in the middle. What do you suppose is in the middle of a third class lever?

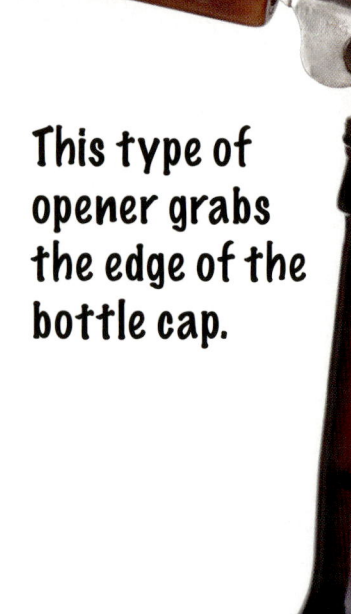

This type of opener grabs the edge of the bottle cap.

This type of opener has a pointed tip, or wedge, that pierces the top of the can.

17

THIRD CLASS LEVERS

Third class levers have the effort between the fulcrum and the load. They are actually quite common. In fact, when you lifted this book, you used a third class lever. When you lift an object, the load is in your hand, the effort is the muscle in your lower arm, and the fulcrum is your elbow!

LOAD

EFFORT

If the little girl uses enough effort the load, or piñata, just might hit the onlookers.

19

DOUBLE LEVERS

Other third class levers include tweezers and tongs, which are double levers, too. Double levers have two strong bars that come together at the fulcrum. Imagine using tongs to grab a hot dog. Where are the load, effort, and fulcrum?

A double second-class lever has two bars joined by a fulcrum, but the load lies in the middle, not at one end like the hot dog. A nutcracker is a double second-class lever! You place the nut (the load) in the center. You apply force at one end and the hinge acts as the fulcrum at the opposite end.

FORCE

LOAD

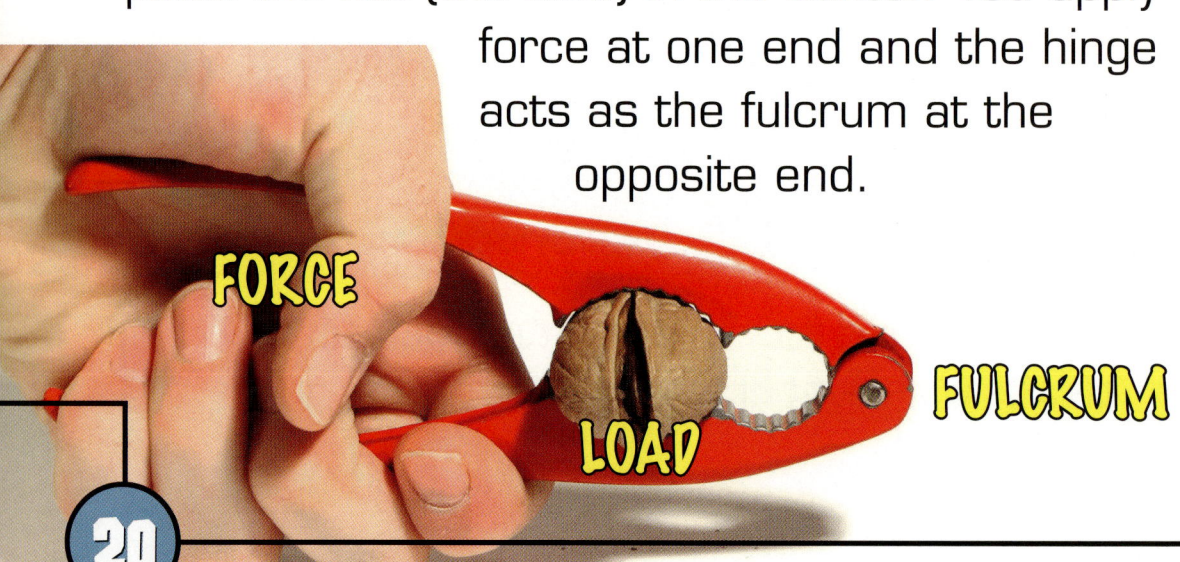

FULCRUM

Tweezers are levers that help us grasp tiny objects.

21

INDEX

can opener(s)   4, 8, 16
complex machines   6
first class lever(s)   12, 16, 22
mechanical advantage   8
nutcracker   20
scissors   22
second class lever(s)   14, 16, 20
seesaw   12
third class lever(s)   16, 18, 19, 20, 22
tongs   20
tweezers   20
wheelbarrow   14

WEBSITES TO VISIT

www.kidskonnect.com/content/view/99/27/
www.edheads.org/activities/simple-machines/
www.brainpop.com/technology/simplemachines/

ABOUT THE AUTHORS

David and Patricia Armentrout specialize in nonfiction children's books. They enjoy exploring different topics, and have written on a variety of subjects, including communities, sports, animals, and people. David and Patricia love to spend their free time outdoors with their two boys and dog Max.